CUT LUV
PAPERS

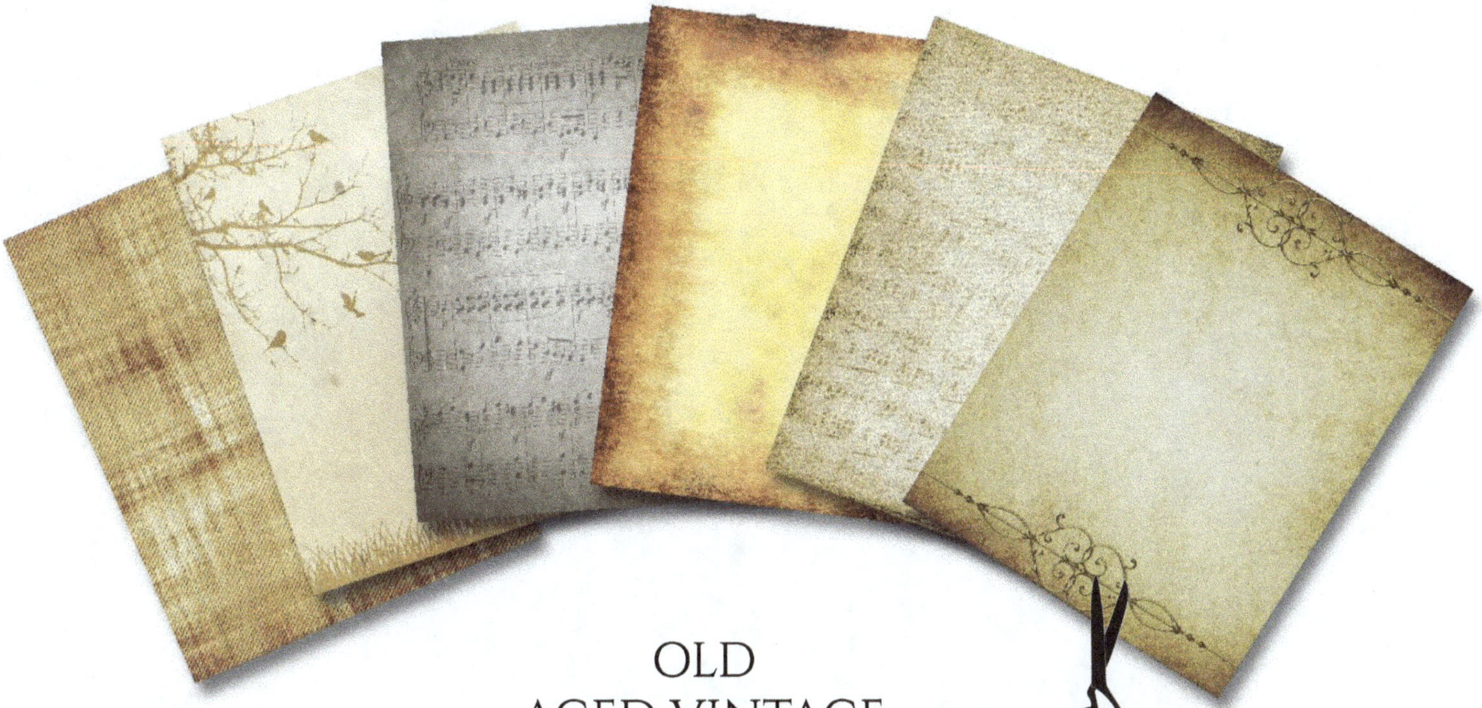

OLD
AGED VINTAGE
DECORATIVE CRAFT PAPER
8.5 x 11 | 12 SHEETS

REMOVE WITH SCISSORS

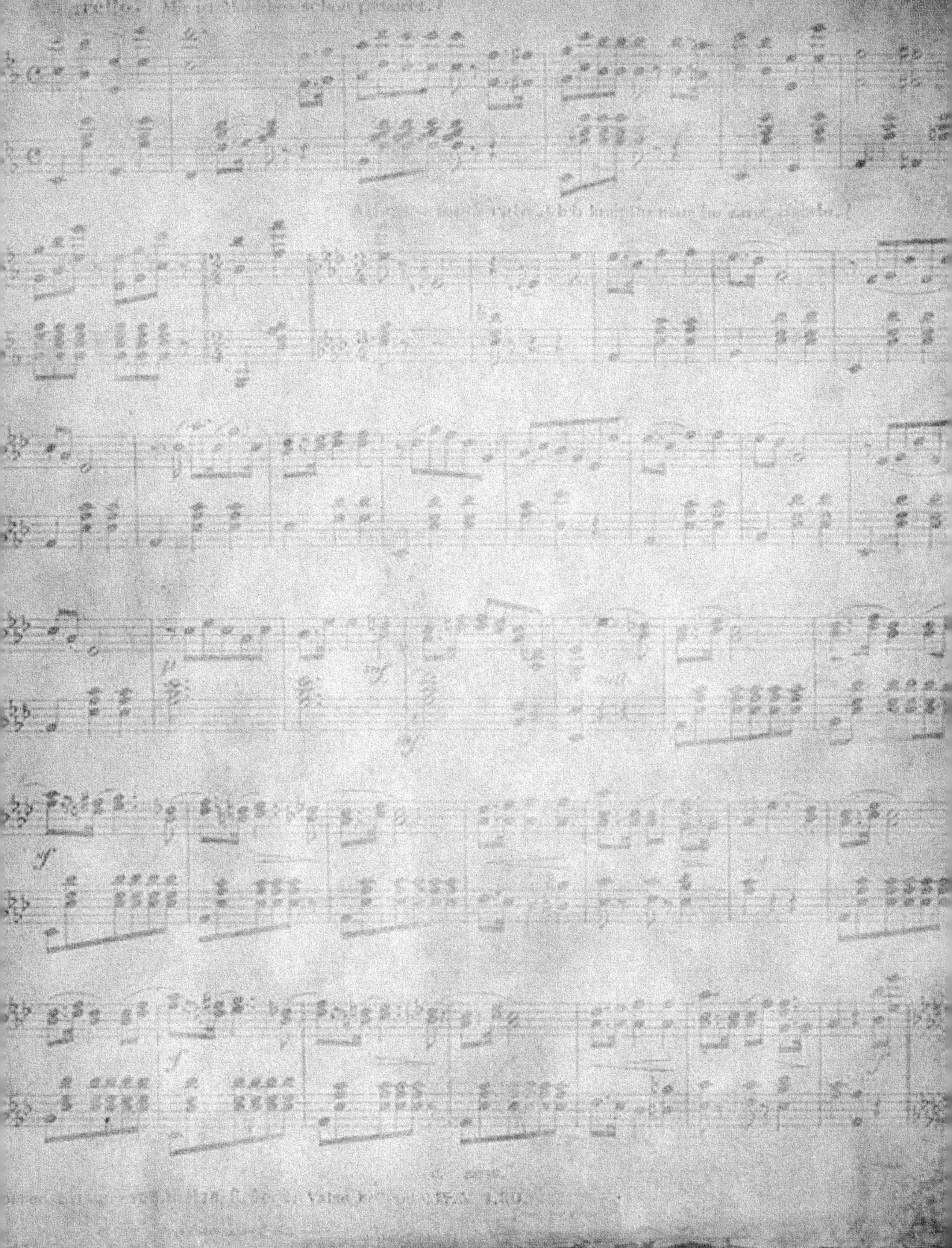

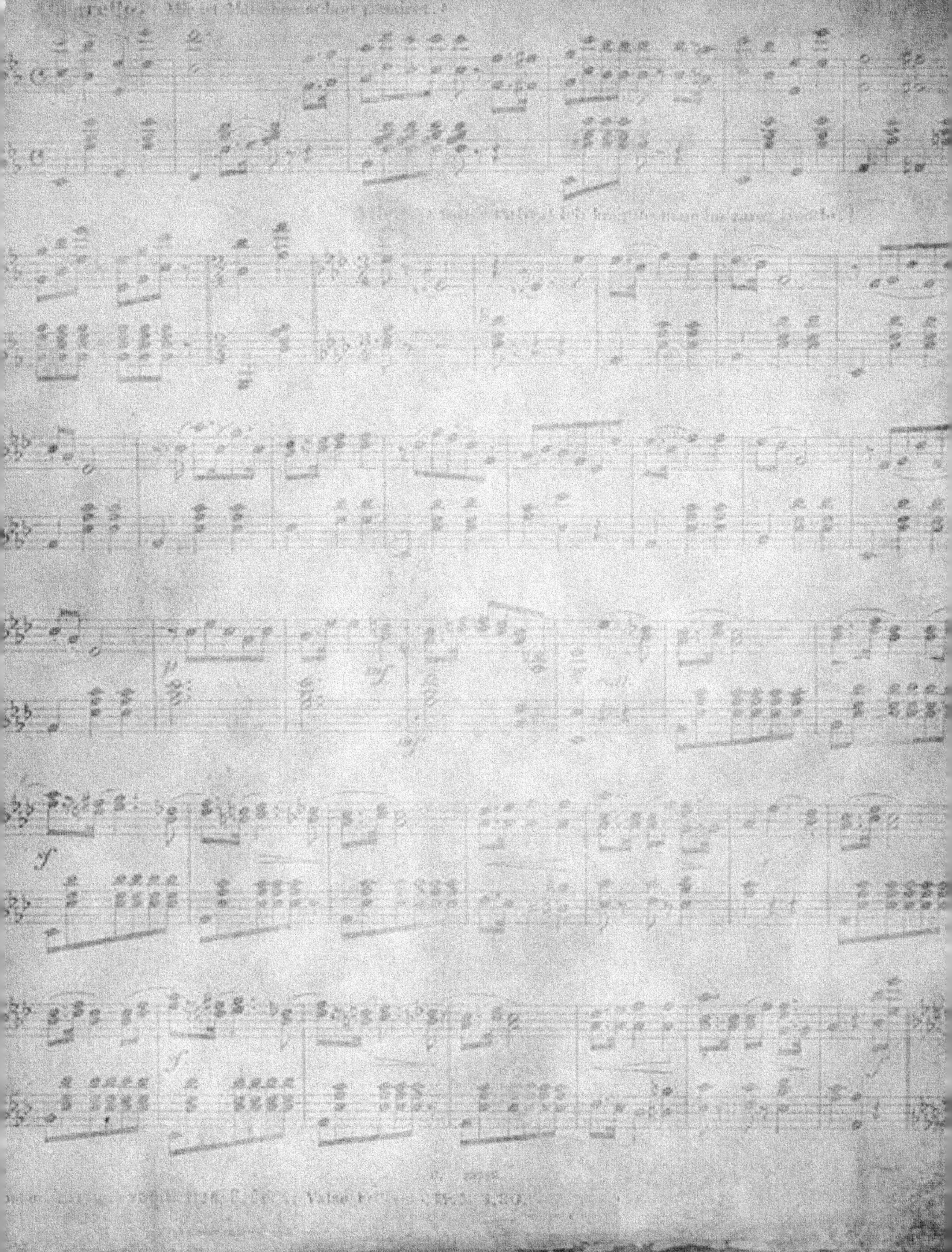

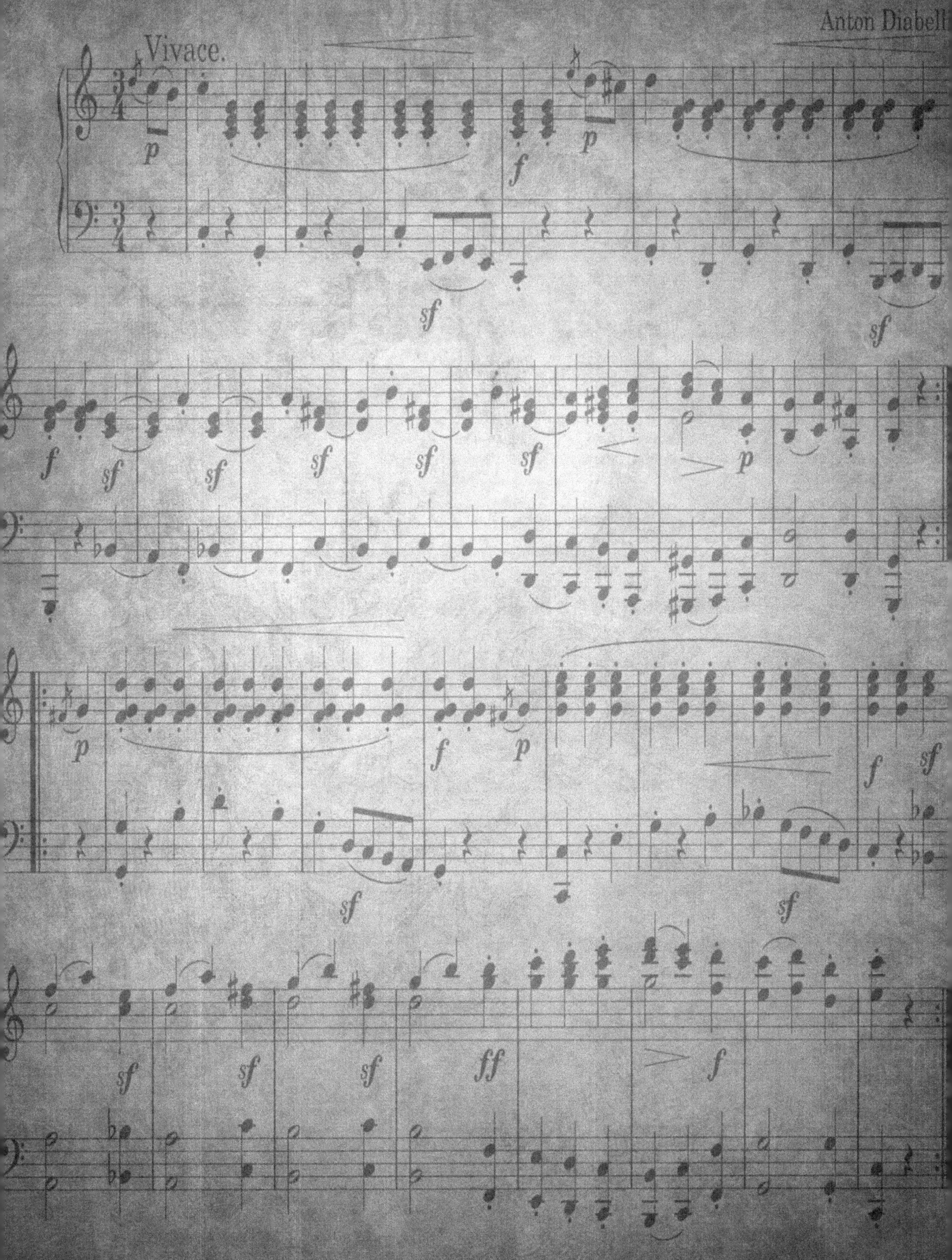
Vivace.
Anton Diabelli

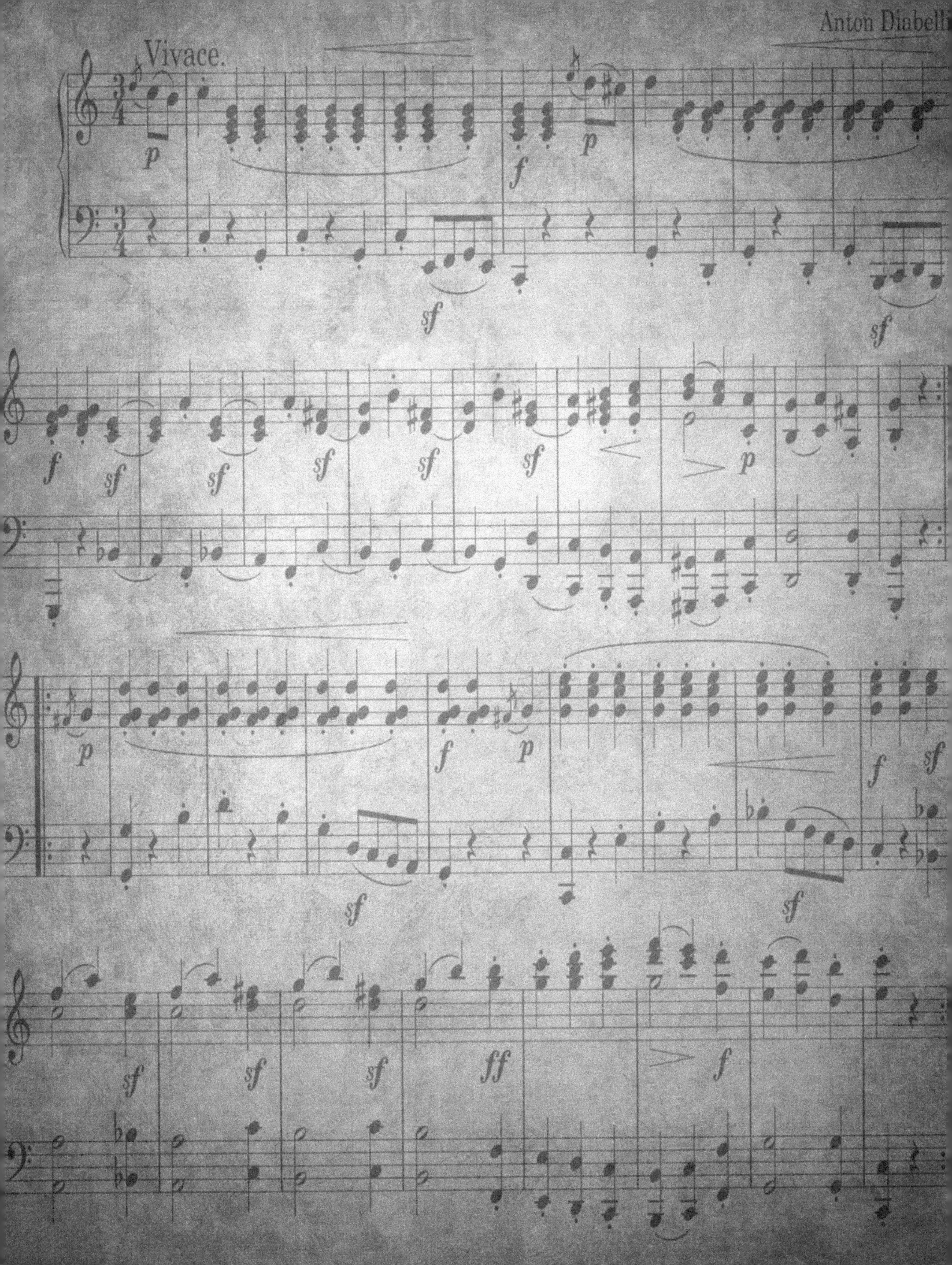
Anton Diabelli
Vivace.